SUSAN B. ANTHONY'S WOMEN'S RIGHT TO SUFFRAGE SPEECH

FRONT SEAT OF HISTORY: FAMOUS SPEECHES

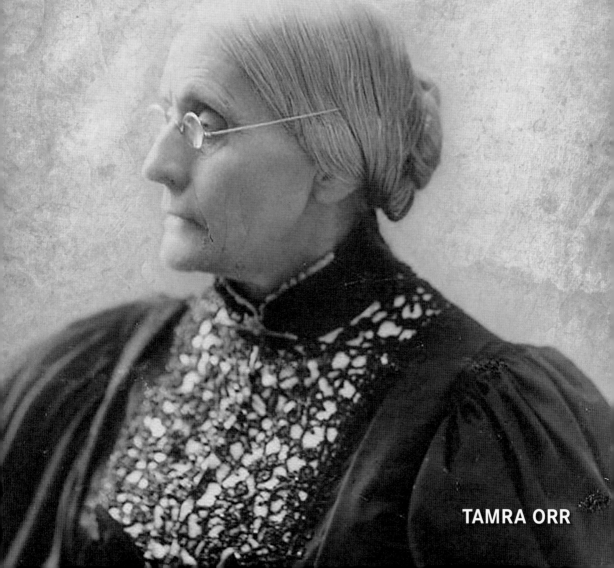

TAMRA ORR

CHERRY LAKE PRESS

Published in the United States of America by Cherry Lake Publishing Group
Ann Arbor, Michigan
www.cherrylakepublishing.com

Reading Adviser: Marla Conn, MS, Ed., Literacy specialist, Read-Ability, Inc.
Content Adviser: Adam Fulton Johnson, PhD, Assistant Professor, History, Philosophy, and Sociology of Science, Michigan State University
Photo credits: © Library of Congress, LC-USZ62-111423, cover; © Library of Congress, LC-DIG-ggbain-10997, 5; © Library of Congress, LC-DIG-hec-03677, 6; © Library of Congress, LC-DIG-hec-30267, 8; © Library of Congress, LC-USZ62-114833, 9; © Library of Congress, LC-USZ62-135533, 10; © Library of Congress, LC-USZ62-30776, 13; © Everett Historical/Shutterstock.com, 14, 20, 28 [bottom], 29 [bottom]; © Library of Congress, LC-USZ61-791, 16; © U.S. Information Agency/The U.S. National Archives, 7452469, 19; © Sipa USA/AP Images, 23; © Aimee Fawn/Alamy Stock Photo, 24; © Library of Congress, LC-USZ62-10761, 25; © Sheila Fitzgerald/Shutterstock.com, 26; © Library of Congress, LC-DIG-npcc-01204, 28 [top]; © duncan1890/iStock.com, 29 [top]

Cherry Lake Press is an imprint of Cherry Lake Publishing Group.

Library of Congress Cataloging-in-Publication Data
Names: Orr, Tamra, author.
Title: Susan B. Anthony's women's right to suffrage speech / by Tamra Orr.
Description: Ann Arbor, Michigan : Cherry Lake Publishing, 2021 | Series: Front seat of history: famous speeches | Includes index. | Audience: Grades 4-6
Identifiers: LCCN 2020005699 (print) | LCCN 2020005700 (ebook) | ISBN 9781534168794 (hardcover) | ISBN 9781534170476 (paperback) | ISBN 9781534172319 (pdf) | ISBN 9781534174153 (ebook)
Subjects: LCSH: Anthony, Susan B. (Susan Brownell), 1820-1906—Oratory—Juvenile literature. | Feminists—United States—Biography—Juvenile literature. | Suffragists—United States—Biography—Juvenile literature. | Women's rights—United States—History—Juvenile literature. | Women—Suffrage—United States—History—Juvenile literature.
Classification: LCC HQ1413.A55 O78 2021 (print) | LCC HQ1413.A55 (ebook) | DDC 305.42092 [B]—dc23
LC record available at https://lccn.loc.gov/2020005699
LC ebook record available at https://lccn.loc.gov/2020005700

Cherry Lake Publishing Group would like to acknowledge the work of the Partnership for 21st Century Learning, a Network of Battelle for Kids. Please visit http://www.battelleforkids.org/networks/p21 for more information.

Printed in the United States of America
Corporate Graphics

ABOUT THE AUTHOR

Tamra Orr is the author of more than 500 nonfiction books for readers of all ages. A graduate of Ball State University, she now lives in the Pacific Northwest with her family. When she isn't writing books, she is either camping, reading or on the computer researching the latest topics.

TABLE OF CONTENTS

"The Woman Who Dared"

In November 1872, Susan B. Anthony, three of her sisters, and several friends walked into a barbershop in Rochester, New York, and registered to vote. It was illegal for women to vote at the time, but she was a **suffragette** and believed that this law was unjust. Four days later, the women voted for the first time. Their victory was short-lived. They were all arrested and fined $100—equal to more than $2,000 today. On January 24, 1873, Anthony was charged with "knowingly, wrongfully, and willingly" voting even though it was illegal. Her trial was set for June 17, 1873. She knew she had a lot of work to do before that day rolled around.

Rosalie Gardiner Jones (center), called General Jones by fellow suffragettes, organized many marches.

"Oh for goodness' sake!" exclaimed Mr. Thomason. "This is getting ridiculous."

Henry's ears perked up at the sound of his father's tone. He watched him from the sitting room.

"What's wrong, dear?" Mrs. Thomason asked, making her way out of the kitchen.

FOR WOMEN
PROCESSION
AYETTE SQUARE TO CAPITOL
TURDAY MAY 9
STARTS 3 P. M.
PRECEDED BY
EETING BELASCO TH
75¢ 50¢ 25¢ | 12.30 O'CLOCK P.M. | REGISTER
F ST

Suffragettes advertised marches and events.

"Come and look at this cartoon in *The Daily Graphic*,"
Mr. Thomason replied, pointing to a drawing on the newspaper's
front page. Mrs. Thomason leaned over to study the drawing.
Shaking her head, she muttered, "Oh my." But, as she headed back
to the kitchen, Henry was sure he saw the corners of her mouth
twitch. Now he was curious.

Henry peered over at his father's newspaper and gulped. It featured a cartoon labeled "The Woman Who Dared." It showed Susan B. Anthony in a too-short skirt, wearing men's boots underneath. Henry knew from school that Ms. Anthony was fighting for women's right to vote.

It was the rest of the cartoon that was the most shocking, though. In the background, men were carrying babies and grocery sacks. A woman wore a police officer's uniform. No wonder his father was so upset.

"Why in the world does this Anthony woman want to vote in the first place?" Mr. Thomason wondered. "Why doesn't she just stay home like you, Margaret?" he added, looking toward his wife. "Her trial begins in less than 2 weeks. Then this entire problem will just go away!"

Suffragettes hang a flag in front of the National Woman's Party Headquarters in Washington, DC.

Although his mother nodded and smiled, Henry could tell she was upset by what his father said. He suspected there were things she would like to say, but didn't.

That evening, when his mother stopped in his room to say good night, Henry was waiting.

"What do you think of Miss Anthony and her suffragettes?" he asked.

Not everyone supported the cause of women's suffrage.

"Why do you ask?" Mrs. Thomason murmured, tucking in the sheets around him.

"Everyone's talking about her," replied Henry. "Why would she fight for the right to vote if it means she could go to jail?"

"I think Miss Anthony has some very important ideas that we should listen to with an open mind," Mrs. Thomason answered. "For now, get some sleep."

As Henry closed his eyes, he decided that he would search out Anthony's next speech. He wanted to hear what she had to say.

A Press Divided

Anthony's arrest and upcoming trial were all over the newspapers at the time. Newspaper editors were divided based on their political party's opinions. **Republicans** believed that the battle for the right to vote was understandable and eventually would be achieved. But **Democrats** thought the suffragettes displayed "female lawlessness."

CHAPTER 2

"Friends and Fellow Citizens"

Henry grinned—he had done it! He heard that Susan B. Anthony was speaking in a park near where he lived. So he headed straight there in hopes of hearing her. His timing was perfect. Anthony was standing up and just starting to speak. She was a serious-looking woman. She stood tall in a gray silk dress. A white lace collar encircled her throat. Her hair was pulled back tightly, making her look that much more serious and important.

In 1913, the Woman Suffrage Party in Ohio had around 4,000 members.

The Seneca Falls convention in New York is said to have launched the suffrage movement in the United States.

"Friends and fellow citizens," she began. She explained that she had been arrested for voting in the last election. And she was going to prove to everyone that she had not committed a crime. Instead, Anthony claimed, she had simply exercised her citizen's rights, guaranteed to all United States citizens by the U.S. Constitution.

[21ST CENTURY SKILLS LIBRARY]

"Exactly what does the Constitution say about voting?" someone behind Henry whispered. He had been wondering that too.

"The **preamble** of the federal Constitution says . . . It was we, the people—not we, the white male citizens, nor yet we, the male citizens—but we, the whole people, who formed the Union," Anthony pointed out. "And we formed it, not to give the blessings of liberty, but to secure them, not to the half of ourselves and the half of our **posterity**, but to the whole people, women as well as men."

Henry saw some people in the audience nodding. Others looked angry. Henry knew that the preamble to the Constitution used the phrase "we the people." And people, he figured, were not just men, no matter what the Founding Fathers meant.

Anthony met Elizabeth Cady Stanton in 1851.

Anthony continued to speak. "For any state to make sex a qualification that must ever result in the **disfranchisement** of an entire half of the people is a violation of the supreme law of the land. The blessings of liberty are forever withheld from women."

Henry had more questions about women's rights. He had some serious thinking to do.

Born into Rebellion

Susan Brownell Anthony was a rebel almost from birth. Her parents Daniel and Lucy were **abolitionists**, *and her family was also part of the* **temperance movement**. *After Anthony was denied the right to speak at a convention because she was a woman, she decided to join the women's rights movement. She and Elizabeth Cady Stanton co-founded the National Woman Suffrage Association. When the 19th Amendment passed 14 years after her death, it was nicknamed the "Susan B. Anthony Amendment" in her honor.*

CHAPTER 3

"The Only Question"

But Susan B. Anthony was not done. She continued, "The only question left to be settled here is, are women persons? And I hardly believe any of our opponents will have the hardihood [nerve] to say they are not!"

Were women people? Henry asked himself. Well, of course they were. But women were often treated differently than men. Henry had always been told that women were weaker and not as smart. He was starting to realize that these beliefs were not fair. Why had he never thought about them before?

During the New York Shirtwaist Strike of 1909, women factory workers, and woman suffrage supporters, picketed for better working conditions.

He pictured the women he saw regularly: his teacher, his mother, his grandmother, and his friends. They did seem different than he was, but not less human. His friend Martha was definitely faster at math than he was. His mother worked just as hard as his father and could do strong things, like bring in firewood every morning. Sometimes she even brought in more than his father! So, why were women being treated differently by the government?

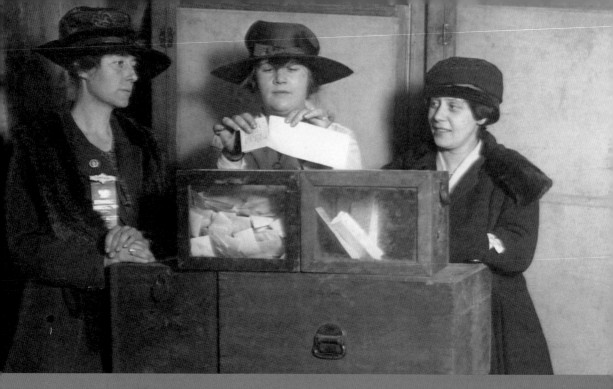

Before the 19th Amendment, suffragists would vote illegally in protest.

Anthony was speaking again. "Being persons, then, women are citizens; and no state has a right to make any new law, or enforce any old law, that shall **abridge** their privileges or immunities. Hence, every **discrimination** against women in constitutions and laws of the several states is today null and void."

Over the next few weeks, Henry reflected often on Anthony's words and the questions they raised.

Then one night at dinner, Mr. Thomason announced, "See, the jury found Anthony guilty! She has been fined $100."

Both he and Henry were surprised when Mrs. Thomason fired back, "Well, of course they did! It was an all-male jury! They had no choice. Judge Hunt instructed them to find her guilty. They did not even get to vote on it. How is that possibly fair?"

For the next several weeks, Henry saw many stories in the newspaper about Anthony's trial. Some editors felt that the judge's decision was fair, but others considered it illegal. One story stated that "Miss Anthony had no trial by jury. She had only a trial by Judge Hunt. This is not what the Constitution guarantees."

Henry began to wonder if the day would ever come when women would get the right to vote.

The 19th Amendment

The fight for women's right to vote began in 1848 with a convention held in Seneca Falls, New York. Women like Susan B. Anthony, Elizabeth Cady Stanton, and Lucretia Mott could never have imagined it would take until 1920 for the 19th Amendment to finally be **ratified**. *After that, on November 2, 1920, 8 million women voted in the United States for the first time.*

A Trip to Mount Hope

"I'm so glad I get to vote this year," Lindsay said. She had just turned 18 a few days earlier, and this was her first election. She had read multiple online articles about the candidates. She was ready to cast her vote for the one she thought would do the best job.

"I'm proud of you," Lindsay's mother said. "Voting is such an important right for all Americans."

When they reached the polling station, Lindsay and Mrs. Brown came to a halt. The line of voters snaked out of the building and around the street corner. "This is going to take hours," complained Lindsay. She was excited to vote but did not want to spend her entire morning standing in line.

In 2019, more women than ever were elected into government offices.

"Hold on," Mrs. Brown replied. "Look, it's a gorgeous autumn morning in New York. I even brought snacks." She reached into her purse and pulled out two granola bars. "Voting is important enough to wait for."

Lindsay realized her mother was right. Between nibbling on their granola bars, chatting with other people, and just enjoying

Susan B. Anthony was buried at Mount Hope Cemetery in 1906.

the morning sunshine, time flew by faster than either of them had expected.

As the two women walked out of the voting booth, they were handed stickers proclaiming, "I Voted!"

"Cool," Lindsay said, placing the sticker on her chest. "Now I can show off all day."

"Actually," said Mrs. Brown with a grin, "I have another idea. Come with me."

[21ST CENTURY SKILLS LIBRARY]

A collection of "votes for women" buttons shows the types of buttons worn during the women's suffrage movement.

Today's women's movement focuses on including all women, regardless of race or identity, in the fight for justice.

By the time they reached the Mount Hope Cemetery, Lindsay was totally confused.

"Lindsay, do you remember reading about Susan B. Anthony in school?" Mrs. Brown asked.

"She dedicated her entire life to getting women the right to vote," Lindsay replied, nodding.

"It is thanks to her hard work and her fellow suffragettes that you have the privilege to vote today," her mother said. She pointed to a nearby gravestone. It was covered in "I Voted!" stickers. "Let's show her our gratitude," Mrs. Brown added.

As Lindsay added her sticker to the others, she whispered a "thank-you" to "the woman who dared."

Now a Majority

Women have become the majority of voters in state and local elections. Research shows that women cast between 4 million and 7 million more votes than men do in these elections. In 2018, more women were elected into public office than ever before. Anthony said, "There never will be complete equality until women themselves help to make laws and elect lawmakers."

1872
Anthony is arrested for illegally voting in Rochester, New York, but continues to travel throughout the country making speeches.

1852
Anthony attends her first women's rights convention.

1850

1860

1870

1851
Susan B. Anthony meets Elizabeth Cady Stanton.

1873
Anthony's trial begins, and she is found guilty.

1863
Anthony and Stanton write "Appeal to the Women of the Republic" and together found the Women's National Loyal League, which supports a constitutional amendment to end slavery.

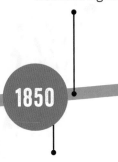

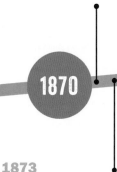

CHARACTER SKETCHES AT THE WOMEN'S SUFFRAGE MEETING AT ST. JAMES'S HALL

1906
Anthony dies at the age of 86.

1880

1890

1900

1881
Anthony and others publish volumes
in *History of Woman Suffrage*.

Speech Highlight

"It was we, the people—not we, the white male citizens, nor yet we, the male citizens—but we, the whole people, who formed the Union. And we formed it, not to give the blessings of liberty, but to secure them, not to the half of ourselves and the half of our posterity, but to the whole people, women as well as men. And it is downright mockery to talk to women of their enjoyment of the blessings of liberty while they are denied the use of the only means of securing them provided by this democratic-republican government [the ballot]."

Read the full speech at https://voicesofdemocracy.umd.edu/anthony-is-it-a-crime-speech-text.

Research and Act

Susan B. Anthony dedicated her life to the idea of equality. She worked hard for the world to see women as equals and deserving the same rights as men. She also spoke a great deal about the plight of slaves and former slaves in the country.

Research
Research how the suffrage movement and the abolition movement often overlapped. What famous figures and political goals did they share? Why did their conferences often combine the two issues?

Act
Draw a Venn diagram to show how suffrage and slavery issues overlapped. Make sure to include what elements were shared and which were unique to each topic. Include speakers, dates, and how each movement achieved its goals.

Further Reading

Colman, Penny. *Elizabeth Cady Stanton and Susan B. Anthony: A Friendship That Changed the World.* New York, NY: Henry Holt and Co., 2011.

Kanefield, Teri. *The Making of America: Susan B. Anthony.* New York, NY: Abrams Books for Young Readers, 2019.

Murphy, Claire. *Marching with Aunt Susan: Susan B. Anthony and the Fight for Women's Suffrage.* Atlanta, GA: Peachtree, 2011.

Pollack, Pam, and Meg Belviso. *Who Was Susan B. Anthony?* New York, NY: Grosset & Dunlap, 2014.

Slade, Suzanne. *Friends for Freedom: The Story of Susan B. Anthony & Frederick Douglass.* Watertown, MA: Charlesbridge, 2014.

GLOSSARY

abolitionists (ab-uh-LISH-uh-nists) people who worked to put an end to slavery

abridge (uh-BRIJ) to shorten by leaving out parts

Democrats (DEM-uh-krats) members of a political party that at the time supported limited government

discrimination (dis-krim-ih-NAY-shuhn) unfair behavior toward others based on differences in things such as race, age, or gender

disfranchisement (dis-FRAN-chize-muhnt) the taking away of someone's legal right, especially the right to vote

posterity (pah-STER-ih-tee) future generations

preamble (PREE-am-buhl) an introductory statement in a constitution

ratified (RAT-uh-fyed) agreed to or officially approved

Republicans (rih-PUHB-lih-kuhnz) members of a political party that at the time supported change and economic reform

suffragette (suhf-rih-JET) a woman who worked to get all women the right to vote

temperance movement (TEMP-ruhns MOOV-muhnt) the effort by people to make the manufacture and sale of alcohol illegal

INDEX